MISSION SURVIVAL:
SAVING EARTH'S ENDANGERED ANIMALS

SAVING THE WHALE

KATHERINE EASON

CHERITON
CHILDREN'S BOOKS

Published in 2026 by **Cheriton Children's Books**
1 Bank Drive West, Shrewsbury, Shropshire SY3 9DJ, UK

First Edition

Author: Katherine Eason
Designer: Paul Myerscough
Editor: Jane Brooke
Proofreader: Ella Newby
Consultant: David Hawksett, BSc

Picture credits: Cover: Shutterstock/Maria T Hoffman. Inside: pp4-5: Shutterstock/Jonas Gruhlke, pp6-7: Shutterstock/Christian Musat, p7b: Shutterstock/Gulf MG, p7c: Shutterstock/Martin Prochazkacz, p8: Shutterstock/Ajit S N, p11: Shutterstock/Martin Prochazkacz, p12: Shutterstock/Amirkhans World, p13b: Shutterstock/Arturo Vigil, p13t: Shutterstock/Tarpan, pp14-15: Shutterstock/SL Photography, pp16-17: Shutterstock/Wongymark1, p17c: Shutterstock/AJP, p17t: Shutterstock/AJP, pp18-19: Shutterstock, p19: Shutterstock/Chanun.V, pp20-21: Shutterstock/Krzysztof Odziomek, p21b: Shutterstock/Wirestock Creators, p21c: Shutterstock/Rob Atherton, p21t: Shutterstock/AbdulSalam453, pp22-23: Shutterstock/Wildestanimal, p23b: Shutterstock/ViDI Studio, p23c: Shutterstock/ViDI Studio, pp24-25: Shutterstock/Martin Prochazkacz, p25: Shutterstock/Scupix, pp26-27: Shutterstock/Imagine Earth Photography, p27b: Shutterstock/Treap News, p27c: Shutterstock/Wildestanimal, p27t: Shutterstock/Ohrim, pp28-29: Shutterstock/Remo Thommen, p28b: Shutterstock/Clare Louise Jackson, p29c: Shutterstock/Marian Fil, p29t: Shutterstock/Marian Fil, pp30-31: Shutterstock/Cavan Images, p31: Shutterstock/Mozgova, p32: Shutterstock/James C Farr, p33b: Shutterstock/Rui Duarte, p33t: Shutterstock/Choksawatdikorn, p34: Shutterstock/Alessandro De Maddalena, p34b: Shutterstock/Stockphoto Mania, p34c: Shutterstock/Stockphoto Mania, p35b: Shutterstock/Photofex_AUT, pp36-37: Shutterstock/Lego 19861111, p37b: Shutterstock/Andriy Nekrasov, p38b: Shutterstock/JohnOMultiMedia, p38t: Shutterstock/David Keep, p39b: Shutterstock/Brian Lasenby, pp40-41: Shutterstock/Wildestanimal, p40b: Shutterstock/SpeedKingz, p40c: Shutterstock/SpeedKingz, p42: Shutterstock/CarlosBarquero, p43: Shutterstock/Craig Lambert Photography, p44: Shutterstock/DR Haris, p45: Shutterstock/Marta Masdeu Navarro.

Printed in China

Publisher's Note: The information in the Kids on a Mission features in this book are suggestions for actions that children can take to help protect endangered animals, based on extensive research by the author and consultant. The email addresses and the children featured in the photographs are for illustrative purposes only.

CONTENTS

WHALES IN DANGER

Whales are some of the largest and most mysterious animals in the ocean. They have lived on Earth for millions of years and have **adapted** to life in the sea. Sadly, these majestic creatures are in danger. Because of people, whales may one day become extinct, or die out.

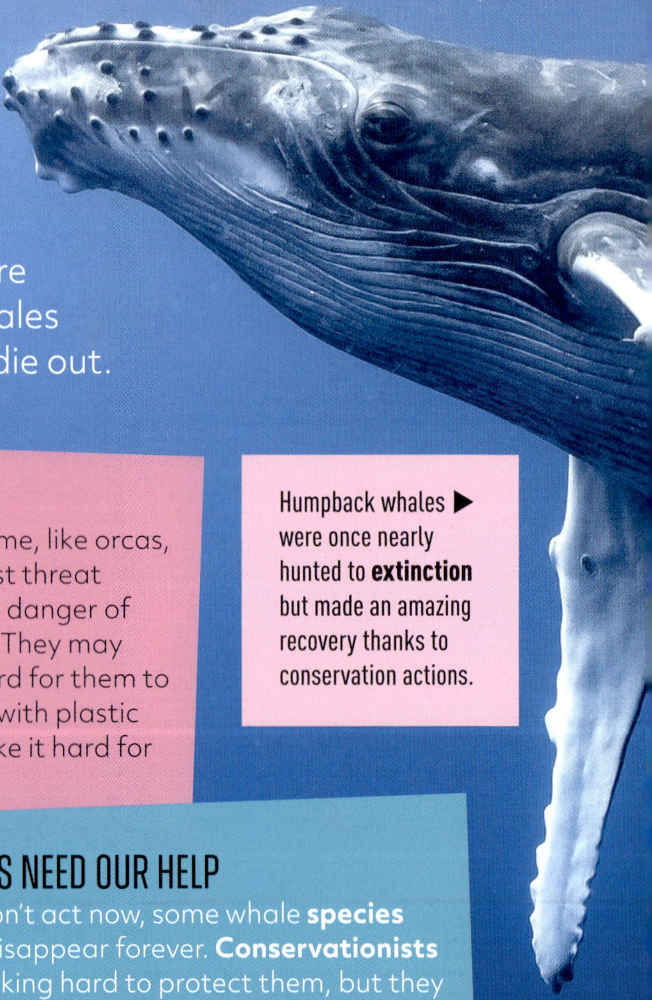

Humpback whales ▶ were once nearly hunted to **extinction** but made an amazing recovery thanks to conservation actions.

THE BIGGEST THREAT

Whales have few natural **predators**. Some, like orcas, may hunt smaller whales, but the biggest threat to whales is from humans. Whales are in danger of being hunted by humans or hit by ships. They may get tangled in fishing nets, making it hard for them to swim. **Pollution** fills their ocean habitat with plastic and harmful chemicals. Loud noises make it hard for them to communicate or find food. These threats, along with the fact that whales **reproduce** slowly, are putting some whale **populations** at risk of extinction.

WHALES NEED OUR HELP

If we don't act now, some whale **species** could disappear forever. **Conservationists** are working hard to protect them, but they need our help. It's up to all of us to make sure whales have a future in our oceans.

The International Union for **Conservation** of Nature (IUCN) keeps a record of the world's species and how at risk of extinction they are. It is called the **Red List.**

There are more than **46,000** animal species on the List.

Many whales are listed as **endangered** or **critically endangered.**

"Whales are giants of the sea, but their gracefulness takes my breath away."

Miriam Rothschild, natural scientist and author

HELP THE WHALE!

There is still hope for whales, and it is not too late to save them. People around the world are working hard to protect these incredible animals. Scientists are studying whales to learn more about them and find ways to keep them safe. Laws are being passed to stop ship strikes and reduce ocean noise. They are being created to protect areas for whales to live in peace. In this book, we'll learn more about whales and why they are in danger. We'll discover how people are helping whales and how some have made it their life's work. We'll also learn how kids everywhere can help protect whales and even explore careers in **marine** conservation. Feeling mission-ready? Then read on!

CHAPTER ONE

MEET THE WHALE

Whales are incredible animals. They spend their whole lives in the ocean, swimming vast distances. Whales have special features that help them survive in the sea.

orca

BIG AND SMALL

Whales come in many sizes. Some species are under 20 feet (6 m) long, while others can grow to over 100 feet (30 m). The blue whale is the largest animal to have ever lived, reaching up to 98 feet (30 m) long and weighing up to 200 tons (203 mt). Their huge size helps them store energy and keep warm in cold waters.

OCEAN BREATHERS

Whales are **mammals**, so they must breathe air. They swim to the surface and breathe out through a special hole called a blowhole on top of their heads. That creates a spout of mist. Their blowhole lets them breathe quickly before diving again. Some whales can hold their breath for over an hour before surfacing to breathe.

TOP TO BOTTOM

Whales have smooth bodies that help them glide through the water. Instead of front legs, they have flippers that help them steer. Their tails, called flukes, move up and down to push them forward. A thick layer of fat, or blubber, helps them stay warm.

DEEP DIVERS

Whales can dive deep to find food. Their ribcage is **flexible**, so it squeezes in safely when they go deep underwater. Their hearts beat more slowly, and their bodies save oxygen, sending it to the most important parts while they hold their breath.

OCEAN MESSAGES

Whales use sound to communicate and find their way. Some species make deep, booming calls that travel for miles. Others use clicks and whistles to find their way and find food. These sounds bounce off objects as an echo. This is called **echolocation**. It helps whales find their way in the darkest depths of the ocean.

In a Group

Scientists group whales based on their features. Whales are part of the *Cetacea* group of animals. They include whales, dolphins, and porpoises. Baleen whales, like humpback whales, have **baleen plates** instead of teeth and feed by filtering tiny creatures from the water. Toothed whales, like orcas and sperm whales, use their teeth to catch fish and squid.

WHERE WHALES LIVE

Whales can be found in every ocean, from the warm waters near the **equator** to the icy polar seas. Some whales prefer deep, open waters, while others stay closer to the coast. Whales can be found in places where there is plenty of food, such as rich feeding areas in the North Atlantic, Pacific, and Southern Oceans.

WONDERS OF THE WHALE WORLD

The two main types of whales include species that are in danger.

Baleen whales
- Rice's whales
- North Atlantic right whales
- North Pacific right whales
- blue whales
- sei whales
- fin whales

Toothed whales
- Perrin's beaked whales
- sperm whales
- some populations of orcas

This map shows where some of ▶ the regional whales can be found.

KEY
- Where beluga whales live
- Where North Pacific right whales live
- Where North Atlantic right whales live
- Where Rice's whales live
- Where Southern right whales live

▲ The majestic blue whale, the largest animal on Earth, is endangered and at risk of dying out.

BIG BLUE HOME

Whales can be found in oceans all around the world. Some species, like the blue whale, travel across whole oceans. The North Atlantic right whale travels between warm waters off the southeastern United States and cooler northern waters where it feeds. Some, like Rice's whale, live in just one special place. This whale is only found in the northeastern Gulf of Mexico. It is **critically endangered** due to oil and gas drilling in its habitat. Only about 50 Rice's whales are left in the wild.

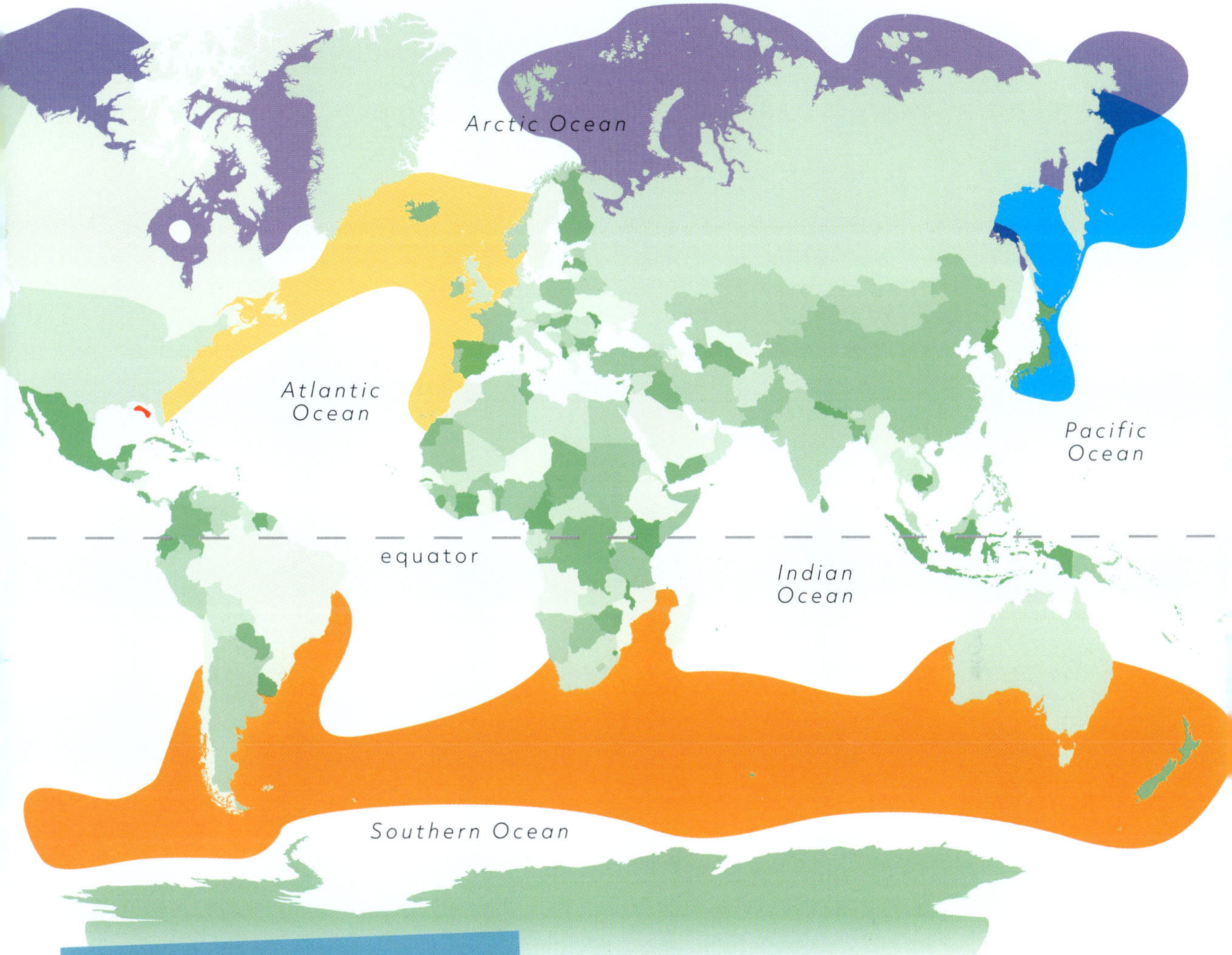

WHALE WANDERERS

Most whales do not stay in one place. Many travel thousands of miles to find food or a place to have their young. These long journeys are called migrations. Humpback whales can travel over 16,000 miles (25,000 km) a year between feeding and breeding areas. Whales have special senses that help them **navigate**. They can sense and use Earth's magnetic field like a compass. This helps them to find their way through the ocean. Whales also use echolocation and the sound of ocean currents to help them find their way during these long migrations.

OCEANS OF CHALLENGES

Whales face many dangers in the ocean. Ship traffic, fishing gear, and ocean noise all put them at risk. Because many whales **migrate** across whole oceans, they often pass through unprotected areas. That means they're more likely to be hit by ships or caught in fishing nets. Some whales, like the North Atlantic right whale, are critically endangered because of these threats. Protecting whales and their ocean homes is important for their survival.

WHY SHOULD WE HELP THE WHALE?

Whales are intelligent creatures that have strong friendships. They are also important animals. In fact, whales are a "keystone species." That means they play a big role in keeping the ocean healthy. Whales help other ocean animals, and they even help people, too!

KEEPING THE OCEAN HEALTHY

Whales are at the top of the **food chain**, helping control numbers of **prey** species and keeping marine ecosystems balanced. For example, whales eat tiny shrimplike animals called krill. If there were too many krill, they could eat too much plankton. That would hurt other animals that need **plankton** to survive. Whale **feces** fertilizes ocean waters, giving plankton the **nutrients** it needs to grow. This helps fish and other sea animals. Even dead whales help other marine animals—when a whale's body sinks, it feeds deep-sea creatures. Healthy whale populations strengthen ocean ecosystems, supporting many species, including fish that people eat.

INTELLIGENT ANIMALS

Whales are intelligent and friendly animals. They live, hunt, and play in groups, and teach their young important skills. Whales show humanlike emotions and have strong bonds with friends and family members. They communicate with clicks, moans, and whistles. Some species, such as sperm whales, orcas, and beluga whales, even have their own special "words". Humpback whales even sing complicated songs that catch on across humpback populations.

◀ As whales dive and swim, they stir up nutrients, helping plankton to grow and keeping the ocean healthy.

What Is an Ecosystem?

An ecosystem is a group of natural parts that all work together for a purpose. Ecosystems include nonliving things such as water, sunshine, and air. These are called abiotic factors. Ecosystems also include living things such as plants and animals. These are called biotic factors. The living things in an ecosystem depend on the abiotic factors in the ecosystem to survive. Every part of the ecosystem has an important part to play. A healthy ecosystem has many different plants and animals living together. If any part of that ecosystem changes or is damaged, the other parts are affected, too.

HUNGRY FEEDERS

Whales spend much of their time searching for food, eating, and resting. Different whale species eat different types of prey.

ON THE MENU

Whales have a varied diet, depending on their species. Some feed on tiny animals like krill and plankton, while others hunt squid, fish, or even mammals such as sea lions. Each species has special adaptations that help it find and catch food. Some follow their prey over long distances, while others stay in one area where there is plenty of food.

FINDING FOOD

Whales use their sharp senses to track down meals. Some whales that feed near the surface rely on their excellent eyesight to find their food. Others dive deep, using echolocation to find prey even in total darkness.

MIGHTY MOUTHS

Baleen whales have comblike plates instead of teeth. They take in large mouthfuls of water and push it out through the baleen, trapping tiny prey such as small fish and krill (shown left) inside. This way of feeding allows them to eat thousands of small animals in one gulp.

TEARING AND MUNCHING

Toothed whales use sharp teeth to grab larger prey such as fish and squid (shown right) and swallow it whole.

PEOPLE ON A MISSION

Whales face many dangers, but they are not alone. Around the world, people are working hard to save whales and to secure a safe future for these majestic creatures. Some dedicate their lives to conservation, making it their mission to help whales survive.

PEOPLE IN OFFICES

Many people who help whales work in offices. Scientists study data to learn more about whale populations. This helps them to make conservation plans. Others work with governments and businesses to make laws and policies that protect whale **habitats**. Conservation organizations raise money to pay for research into whales and programs to rescue them. Communications experts teach people about the threats whales face and actions people can take to protect them.

PEOPLE IN LABS

Scientists such as zoologists and **marine biologists** study whales in labs and research centers. They examine whale bodies and study their diet and health. Their research helps conservationists understand how best to protect whales in the wild.

PEOPLE IN THE OCEANS

Marine biologists, researchers, and wildlife officers work directly in whale habitats. They study whale populations, track their movements, and monitor their health. Some rescue injured whales and work to release them back into the ocean. Wildlife technicians collect data about whales and their **environment**. Public educators and outreach specialists teach people about the threats whales face and how to help them.

▼ Observing whales in their natural habitat helps scientists understand more about these incredible animals.

PEOPLE EVERYWHERE

Everyone can help whales. We can support organizations that protect them. We can learn about their threats and share this knowledge with others. By raising awareness and taking action, we can all play a part in saving whales.

MAKE IT YOUR MISSION

You can help whales and other endangered animals by taking action and planning a career in conservation. Here's how:

1. In this book, you'll discover what actions kids on a mission can take to help whales. Use them to inspire your own actions to protect whales.
2. You'll also discover some of the careers people on a mission have in whale conservation. As you read about each one, think about whether that career in conservation might suit you.
3. At the end of this book, you'll find a guide on how to build a career in conservation. Check it out to discover how you can make saving animals your life mission.

CHAPTER TWO

HOMES UNDER THREAT

Whales rely on healthy, undisturbed habitats to survive. Unfortunately, some of the places where they live, feed, and raise their young are under threat. That puts whales in danger, too.

WATERS UNDER THREAT

Many whales live in deep ocean waters, where they search for food and raise their young. However, human activities are making these waters dangerous. Ships traveling through whale habitats can hit whales, causing serious injuries or even death. Large fishing nets and ropes also trap whales. That makes it hard for them to swim, feed, or surface for air. Noise from ships and underwater drilling fills the ocean. That makes it difficult for whales to communicate with each other or use sound to find their way through the ocean. Oil spills pollute the water, harming both whales and the fish they eat.

HARMING HOMES

Some whales feed near the ocean floor or along the coast. But these feeding areas are being damaged or destroyed. Oil spills and pollution from fish farming poison the water and the food whales rely on. Pieces of plastic and other trash end up in the ocean. Whales may eat this trash by mistake, making them sick or even killing them. Underwater construction along coastal areas and human activities, such as boat traffic, create loud noises that can drive whales away from important feeding areas. Some whales, like Rice's whale, already have small habitats. If those habitats disappear, the whales could too.

◀ Habitat loss and damage are huge threats, especially in coastal and feeding areas where whales rely on healthy ecosystems.

Kids on a Mission

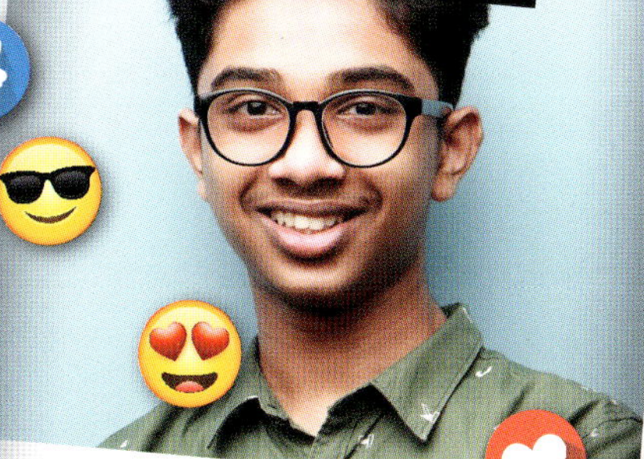

@whalewatcher_06

My family always takes reusable straws, bottles, and bags on days out and we pick up plastic that other people have left behind at the beach. That way, we stop plastic waste ending up in the ocean.

"These noises interfere with whales' ability to feed and navigate, as they rely on sound to 'see' underwater."

Dr Heike Vester, a biologist based in Bodø, Norway

SOMEWHERE SAFE TO LIVE

To help protect whales, conservationists have set up marine protected areas. These are special zones where whales and their habitats should be safe from threats. Scientists study the whales living there and work to reduce dangers like ship strikes, becoming entangled in fishing gear, and noise pollution.

SPOTLIGHT ON POLLUTION

Whales live in vast oceans, but their world is changing. Pollution from plastic, chemicals, and noise is harming these special animals. These threats are making it harder for whales to survive in their ocean home.

MANY DANGERS

Whales face many threats today. Plastic pollution is a big problem. Baleen whales may accidentally swallow tiny pieces of plastic along with their food. Toothed whales may mistake plastic bags for squid or other prey. Tiny plastics, called microplastics, can release harmful chemicals into a whale's body. Large pieces of plastic can block a whale's stomach if eaten. Chemicals from farms, factories, and the military also wash into the ocean. These pollutants can make whales sick and stop them from having healthy babies.

PEOPLE ON A MISSION: WHALE SUPPORT

Scientists and conservationists study whales to understand their behaviors and needs. They also study the dangers whales face. They use special underwater microphones, called hydrophones, to listen to whale sounds and monitor noise pollution. Some scientists work to clean up plastic waste in the ocean. Others study how pollution in the oceans affects the health of whales.

Conservationists push for rules to protect whales. They want to slow ships in whale habitats and reduce ocean noise. Educators teach people about the dangers whales face and how to help. They encourage people to use less plastic and support ocean-friendly activities such as responsible fishing. Whales play a vital role in ocean ecosystems. By protecting them, we can help ensure their survival for **generations** to come.

◀ Rivers carry plastic waste into the ocean where it pollutes marine animals' precious habitats.

▲ Noise from ship engines, drilling, and **military** sonar can be extremely loud. It can even damage whales' hearing. Sudden loud sounds can panic whales and cause them to become **stranded**.

LOSING OUT

The ocean is getting louder. Loud sounds from ships, oil and gas drilling, and **sonar** can be stressful for whales. The noise makes it harder for them to hear and communicate. Whales rely on sound to find food, find their way, and communicate. Noise pollution makes it hard for whales to locate prey or find their way to feeding and breeding areas. It can make the animals confused and lost.

LIVING NEAR THE WHALE

Many different animals live in the ocean. Sadly, some of these amazing creatures are endangered too.

THE MANTA RAY

Manta rays are giant fish with winglike **fins**. They can grow up to 23 feet (7 m) across and weigh as much as 5,300 pounds (2,400 kg). They glide through the ocean and filter tiny plankton from the water as they swim. Manta rays are threatened by overfishing and pollution.

THE VAQUITA

Vaquitas are the world's rarest marine mammals. They are small **porpoises** that grow up to 5 feet (1.5 m) long and weigh about 120 pounds (55 kg). Vaquitas have dark rings around their eyes and mouths. They live only in the northern part of the Gulf of California in Mexico. Fewer than 20 vaquitas remain in the wild. They are often caught in fishing nets meant for other fish. This is called bycatch, and it is their biggest threat.

THE ATLANTIC BLUEFIN TUNA

Atlantic bluefin tuna are strong, fast fish. They can grow up to 10 feet (3 m) long and weigh more than 1,500 pounds (680 kg). They can swim as fast as 43 miles (70 km) per hour. Bluefin tuna are fished for their meat. Overfishing has reduced their numbers.

THE HAWAIIAN MONK SEAL

Hawaiian monk seals grow up to 7.5 feet (2.3 m) long and weigh around 400 pounds (181 kg). These seals live in the warm waters around Hawaii, resting on sandy beaches and rocky shores. They hunt fish, squid, and other food in the ocean. Hawaiian monk seals are endangered due to habitat loss, food shortages, and getting caught in fishing gear.

CHAPTER THREE

UNDER THREAT FROM WHALING

Whaling is the hunting of whales for their blubber, meat, and bones. For many years, people hunted too many whales. Today, whaling is mostly banned, but some whales are still in danger.

▲ Whalers once hunted blue whales and fin whales almost to extinction. If whaling is not stopped, some species, like this fin whale, may disappear forever.

HUNTED FOR OIL AND MEAT

Whales have been hunted for hundreds of years. Their blubber was turned into oil for lamps and machinery. Their meat was eaten, and their bones were used to make tools. By the 1900s, new technology made it easier to hunt whales. Many species were pushed to the edge of extinction.

THE WHALING INDUSTRY

In the 1900s, whaling became a big business. Fast ships and deadly spears called harpoons allowed whalers to catch thousands of whales every year. Blue whales, sei whales, fin whales, and sperm whales were hunted in huge numbers. In 1986, an international ban on whaling was put in place to protect them. But some countries still hunt whales today. Japan, Iceland, and Norway continue to hunt hundreds of whales each year, saying it is part of their culture.

"We need to establish marine protected areas, or 'hope spots', to conserve biodiversity and protect marine life from human activities."

Dr Sylvia Earle, marine biologist and oceanographer

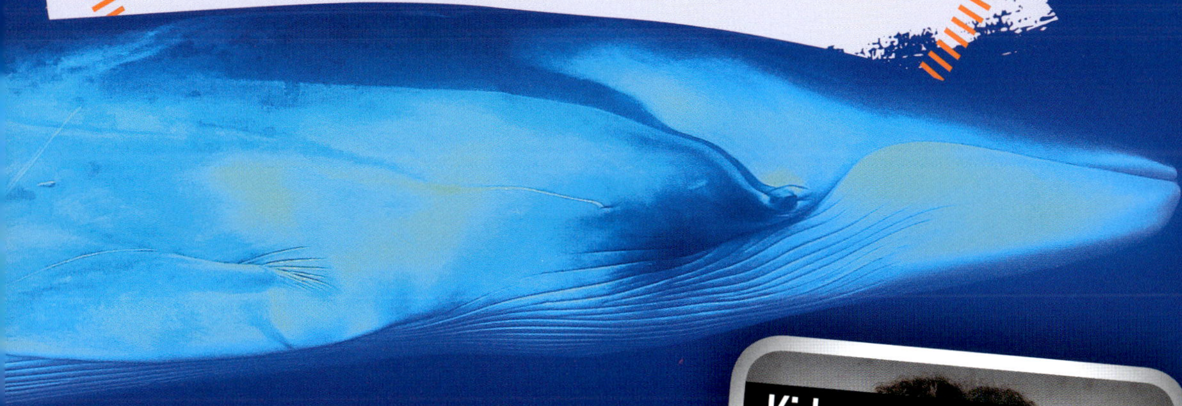

AGAINST THE LAW

The ban on commercial whaling was meant to protect whales from extinction. But illegal whaling still happens. Some whalers secretly kill whales and sell the meat. Others claim to hunt for "scientific research" but then sell the meat. Some whales are caught in fishing nets and taken illegally. Conservationists are working to stop illegal whaling and strengthen protections.

Kids on a Mission

@whale_fan_2009

I signed a petition asking my government to create **marine reserves** where whales and other sea animals will be safe from harm.

SPOTLIGHT ON ILLEGAL WHALING

Today, most countries have banned whaling, but some people still hunt whales illegally. Some whalers operate in secret, while others claim to hunt for research but sell whale meat afterward.

▲ Many endangered whale species, like this sei whale, are still hunted even though their populations are still recovering.

SNEAKY HUNTING

Illegal whaling puts whale populations at risk, especially those still recovering. Some whalers try to hide their activities. They hunt in protected areas or catch more whales than allowed. They use fast boats and powerful harpoons to kill whales quickly before patrols arrive. In some places, whale meat is secretly sold, even though it is illegal. Many illegal whalers escape punishment because they hunt in remote ocean areas, far from law enforcement.

DESTROYING FAMILIES

Whaling has had a devastating impact on whale populations, and many have struggled to recover. Because whales reproduce slowly, their numbers don't always recover, even after decades. With fewer whales, it is more difficult for the animals to find mates from different groups. This is important for keeping populations healthy. The loss of one whale affects the whole group. Whales live in close family groups, called pods. When an important family member is killed, it can make it harder for young calves to survive and weaken the whole pod.

▼ Whale-watching helps people learn about whales without harming them.

PEOPLE ON A MISSION: PATROL AND EDUCATE

Conservation groups and governments are working together to stop illegal whaling. Many countries support international agreements, like the International Whaling Commission (IWC), which helps enforce a ban on commercial whaling. Some countries patrol seas where many whales live to ensure these laws are followed. They watch whaling ships and track the number of whales that are being caught. By placing tracking tags on whales to monitor their movements, scientists can check if they are being hunted. Some wildlife groups film illegal hunts and share the evidence with the world. Other groups teach people why protecting whales is important. Awareness campaigns and documentaries are used to teach people about the destruction and enormous harm caused by whaling.

Conservationists also work with local communities to create jobs in tourism instead of whaling. In some places, former whalers now work in whale-watching tourism. This helps protect whales and gives people new jobs. By working together, governments, scientists, and communities can stop illegal hunting and make sure whales are safe for generations to come.

WHALE BABIES

Whale mothers are pregnant for 10 to 18 months, depending on the species. They usually give birth to one baby every two to three years. A baby whale is called a calf. Calves face many dangers in the ocean. Without protection, many do not reach adulthood.

STAYING CLOSE

A whale calf stays close to its mother for protection. She protects her baby from predators like sharks and orcas. She also helps it learn how to swim and dive. A calf will often swim right beside or just underneath its mother for safety. They stay with their mothers for months or even years before they are ready to be on their own.

LOST LESSONS

When older whales are lost, calves lose their protection. They also lose the chance to learn important survival skills. Without these lessons, young whales may struggle to find food and safe habitats, which makes survival even harder.

FIRST BREATH

A whale calf must swim to the surface right after it is born. Its mother gently nudges it upward to take its first breath.

MOTHER'S MILK

A newborn whale drinks milk from its mother. The milk is full of fat, helping the calf grow fast and stay warm in the water. Some calves drink more than 50 gallons (190 l) of milk each day! Calves grow quickly. They can gain over 100 pounds (45 kg) in a day!

A LONG JOURNEY

Some whale mothers and their calves travel thousands of miles together. They migrate from warm waters, where calves are born, to cold feeding areas. The journey can take months. Mother whales teach their young how to survive. They pass down knowledge about migration routes, how to find feeding areas, and dangers to avoid.

CHAPTER FOUR

THE THREAT OF CLIMATE CHANGE

We know that because of climate change, our planet is experiencing more extreme weather patterns. That is having a big impact on habitats, humans, and wildlife such as whales.

▼ Beluga whales depend on their icy habitat for protection from predators such as orca.

WHAT IS CLIMATE CHANGE?

Climate change is a change in temperature or weather in an area over a period of time. Climate change has always happened slowly throughout Earth's history, due to natural factors such as changes in the sun and **geological** activity. However, the climate change we are experiencing today is largely caused by human activities. These include burning fossil fuels, which releases gases into Earth's **atmosphere**. These gases circle the planet like a blanket, causing it to heat up.

▼ Burning **fossil fuels** releases gases, such as carbon dioxide, that make climate change worse. This makes the ocean warmer, changing where whales can find food and threatening their survival.

CHANGING OCEANS

Climate change is making the ocean a harder place for whales to live. Rising temperatures are changing where whales can find food, and melting sea ice is affecting their migration routes. Many whales eat tiny animals that live in cold water, but warming seas are making these food sources harder to find. This means whales have to travel longer distances. At the same time, rising sea levels are changing coastlines where some whales give birth. Also, stronger storms are making the ocean louder. Noise from storms and human activity makes it harder for whales to communicate, hunt for food, and find their way.

Kids on a Mission

@oceanlife_2004

My family don't fly when we go on vacation. Instead, we take a train or carpool. That means we are putting less harmful gases into Earth's atmosphere and protecting the planet from climate change.

"Human threats such as ship strikes, entanglement in fishing gear, and climate change are severely impacting whale populations."

Dr Howard Rosenbaum, director of the Wildlife Conservation Society's Ocean Giants Program

SPOTLIGHT ON WARMING OCEANS

Whales rely on the ocean for food, migration, and survival. But as climate change warms the seas, their way of life is changing. Rising ocean temperatures affect whale habitats, food sources, and migration patterns. Some whales struggle to find enough food, while others face changing environments that make survival harder.

WARMER WATERS, CHANGING FOOD SUPPLIES

Oceans absorb much of the heat from climate change. This is a problem for many sea creatures, including whales. Many whales eat tiny sea creatures called copepods. These creatures need cold water to survive. As the ocean warms, copepods are becoming harder to find, and whales must travel farther to feed. That takes more energy, leaving them weak. Warmer waters also affect fish populations that whales depend on, changing where and when they migrate. Some whales arrive at their feeding areas only to find that their food is no longer there.

PEOPLE ON A MISSION: FIGHTING CLIMATE CHANGE

Many scientists are studying how rising ocean temperatures are affecting whales. Some researchers are tracking whale movements to see how rising temperatures are changing their migration routes. Efforts to reduce ship strikes and entanglement in fishing gear along these routes are critical.

Other researchers study how food sources are changing because of warming waters. They want to understand what that means for whale survival. By learning more, they hope to find ways to help whales survive in a changing world.

Marine reserves and protected areas help safeguard whale habitats. Some marine conservationists are working to protect important feeding and breeding areas. Others are pushing for policies to reduce **carbon emissions**, the main cause of climate change.

People around the world are raising awareness about climate change and its impact on whales. Protecting these animals means protecting the oceans they call home.

▲ A group of scientists take samples and measure melting **glacier** water in Antarctica. Understanding the threats caused by climate change is key to protecting whales and their ocean home.

▲ Krill numbers are dropping because of rising sea temperatures and melting sea ice. That makes it hard for blue, fin, and humpback whales (seen here) to find enough krill to eat.

WHALES NEED OPEN OCEAN

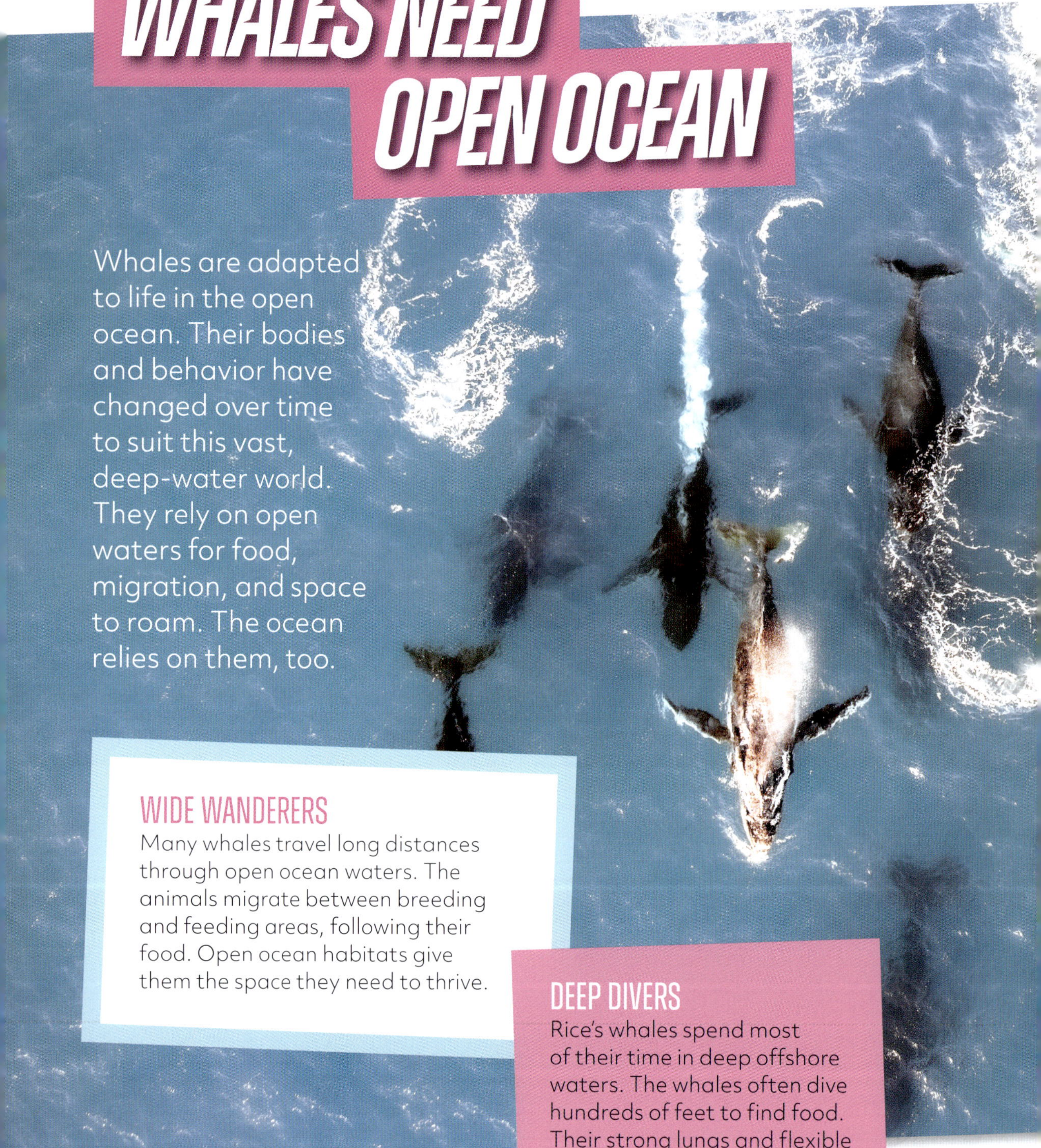

Whales are adapted to life in the open ocean. Their bodies and behavior have changed over time to suit this vast, deep-water world. They rely on open waters for food, migration, and space to roam. The ocean relies on them, too.

WIDE WANDERERS

Many whales travel long distances through open ocean waters. The animals migrate between breeding and feeding areas, following their food. Open ocean habitats give them the space they need to thrive.

DEEP DIVERS

Rice's whales spend most of their time in deep offshore waters. The whales often dive hundreds of feet to find food. Their strong lungs and flexible ribcage help them survive these deep dives.

OCEAN FEEDERS

Baleen whales, like sei whales and right whales, eat tiny creatures called zooplankton (left). They use baleen plates in their mouths like a strainer to trap food as they swim. Some whales, like right whales, travel between feeding areas. Others, like sei whales, follow their prey around the ocean. These whales need to travel over large distances to find enough food to eat.

HEALTHY OCEANS

Whales help keep the ocean healthy. They stir up nutrients when they dive and surface, which helps feed tiny ocean plants. Their waste also provides nutrients for the ocean's food chain. Every part of the ocean is connected, and whales play an important role in keeping it balanced.

CHAPTER FIVE

OTHER THREATS TO WHALES

The whales that survive the dangers of ship strikes, climate change, hunting, pollution, and ocean noise also face other threats. These magnificent marine mammals are also affected by overfishing and other human activities.

THE PROBLEM WITH OVERFISHING

Every year, millions of tons of fish are taken from the ocean, upsetting the delicate balance of marine life. Many whales depend on krill, small fish, and squid to survive. When too many are caught, whales struggle to find enough to eat. As fish populations drop and fish farms grow, whales are finding it harder to find food. In some areas, overfishing forces whales to search for food in new places, where they face even more risks, such as busy shipping lanes.

Kids on a Mission

@emily4whales-05

I asked my parents to only buy **sustainable** seafood to protect the food chains whales rely on.

"Most of the damage suffered by the ocean has been caused by overfishing, pollution, and destruction of habitats. If we tackle these problems now, we buy ourselves time to work on climate change."

Dr Nancy Knowlton, marine biologist and coral reef expert

TROUBLE FROM FISH FARMS

Fish farming, or marine aquaculture, is another growing problem. These farms pollute the ocean with waste and chemicals, harming the ecosystems that whales depend on. Some are built in important whale habitats, blocking the paths whales have used for centuries. Some fisheries also use loud underwater equipment, driving whales away from important feeding areas.

▲ Fish farms pollute the ocean and disrupt whale habitats. Overfishing and fish farming are changing the ocean habitat in ways that put whales at risk.

▲ This orca is hunting for herring near a fishing boat in Norway.

SPOTLIGHT ON ENTANGLEMENT

Industrial fishing doesn't just take food from whales—it also puts them in danger. Entanglement is when whales get trapped in fishing gear like nets, ropes, or lines floating in the ocean. Entanglement in fishing gear is one of the biggest threats to whales, often causing serious injury or death.

The North Atlantic right whale is ▶ critically endangered, with less than 400 left in the wild. In the past, these whales were hunted almost to extinction. Today, many die from ship strikes and getting tangled in fishing gear.

WHALES IN TROUBLE

Longlines, trawl nets, and lost fishing gear float in the ocean, creating deadly traps that whales can get tangled in. Once caught, they struggle to break free, but the fishing gear can wrap around their fins, tails, or mouths. That makes it hard to swim, eat, or surface for air to breathe. Some escape but are left with deep wounds and long-term health problems. Many grow weaker over time, and drown. Strict rules and support for fishermen are key to reducing whale deaths caused by entanglement.

PEOPLE ON A MISSION: WHALE SCIENTISTS

Scientists are working hard to protect whales from entanglement in fishing gear. One way they help is by developing safer fishing methods. Some scientists are testing special ropes that break under a whale's weight, allowing trapped whales to escape. Others are designing "ropeless" fishing gear that uses buoys and the **Global Positioning System (GPS)** instead of long ropes in the water.

Rescue teams also play a big role. When a whale gets tangled, trained experts rush to help. Using boats and special tools, they carefully cut away the fishing gear to free the whale. Scientists study these cases to understand where and how entanglements happen, helping prevent future accidents.

Conservation groups work with governments to make rules and laws to protect whales. They also work with fishers to find ways to protect both whales and fishermen. Some areas have seasonal fishing controls to keep whales safe when they pass through.

Public awareness is important, too. People are learning more about the dangers of entanglement and how to support safer fishing practices. With teamwork, new technology, and better protections, conservationists and scientists are giving whales a better chance to live free from these deadly threats.

▼ It is estimated that about 640,000 tons (650,000 mt) of fishing gear is lost or thrown away into the oceans every year.

OTHER MARINE MAMMALS IN DANGER

Whales are not the only ocean animals under threat. In many of Earth's oceans, other marine mammals are also in danger.

THE SEA OTTER

Sea otters live along the coasts of the North Pacific Ocean. They have the thickest fur of any animal, which keeps them warm in cold water. Sea otters grow up to 5 feet (1.5 m) long and weigh around 100 pounds (45 kg). They float on their backs and use rocks to crack open shellfish. Sea otters are endangered due to oil spills, habitat loss, and entanglement in fishing gear.

THE MANATEE

Manatees are large, slow-moving marine mammals. They can grow up to 13 feet (4 m) long and weigh over 1,300 pounds (590 kg). Manatees live in warm, shallow waters and eat seagrass. They are sometimes called "sea cows." Manatees are endangered because of habitat destruction, boat strikes, and pollution, which harms the seagrass they rely on for food.

THE GALÁPAGOS SEA LION

The Galápagos sea lion is a playful marine mammal found only around the Galápagos Islands. It can grow up to 8 feet (2.4 m) long and weigh over 550 pounds (250 kg). These sea lions rest on sandy beaches and rocky shores. They hunt fish and squid in the ocean. They are threatened by pollution, habitat loss, and food shortages caused by climate change.

WHAT'S NEXT FOR THE WHALE?

No one knows for sure what the future holds for whales. Some live in protected areas where they are safe from danger, but many swim far beyond these safe zones. Even with laws to protect them, whales still face big threats. Oceans are becoming busier and louder. Because of climate change, some whales are losing their feeding and breeding grounds as the ocean environment shifts.

HELP FROM CONSERVATIONISTS

People who care about whales can help. Scientists are learning more about where whales go, how they behave, and what they need to survive. They monitor whales' numbers and health. Conservationists use this data to protect the places whales live and reduce the risks they face.

There is hope. Some whale populations that were once nearly wiped out by whaling are now growing once more. This is because people are working hard to protect them.

@Jacob_saves_whales

Adopting a whale through an organization like the Whale and Dolphin Conservation (WDC) or Ocean Conservancy helps support whale conservation groups. I asked my Grandma and Grandad to adopt a whale for me for my birthday.

"The world needs whales, and whales need our protection."

Dr Richard Leakey, conservationist

HELP FROM ORGANIZATIONS

Organizations like the World Wildlife Fund (WWF) and other marine conservation groups are working to protect whales. Some campaign against whaling and keeping whales in captivity. They promote marine protected areas. Others go out in boats to stop whalers. Some organizations enforce laws to protect whales from ship strikes and fishing gear entanglement. They protect whales' habitats and manage whale sanctuaries. Some rescue injured or stranded whales. Organizations also teach people about why whales are important for keeping ocean ecosystems healthy.

◀ Southern right whales are making a comeback thanks to conservation efforts.

HELP FROM ALL OF US

We can all play a part in protecting whales. We can support laws that keep their ocean home safe. We can learn more about whales and share what we know with others. Reducing pollution, especially plastic, can make the ocean a safer place for whales. There is still time to make a difference. If we all work together, we can ensure a future where whales continue to swim in the world's oceans.

MAKE IT YOUR MISSION: A CAREER IN CONSERVATION

Why not make it your mission to build a future career in conservation? That way, you could make a huge difference to whales and other endangered animals. On pages 44–45, you'll find some of the conservation careers that you could pursue. And here are things you can do right now to prepare for a career in conservation and help save whales.

GET SET TO STUDY

If you want a career in conservation, work hard at school now. Pay attention in your science, English, and geography classes. Languages are also useful. If you get a job overseas, being able to speak a foreign language will be very helpful.

Cleaning litter from your local environment ▶ will help protect animals and their habitats.

▼ If you adopt a whale through the WWF, the money you pay will go toward protecting whales and their habitats.

TAKE ACTION!

You have learned about some of the actions that help whales from the Kids on a Mission features in this book. Here are some more ideas for other activities that can help protect whales:

- Adopt a whale! Ask your parents to help you check out the WWF site for information about adopting whales.
- Squid are one of a toothed whale's favorite foods, but squid look a lot like plastic bags. So, bring your own reusable bags when you shop to keep more plastic bags from ending up in oceans.
- Join in or organize beach cleanups. Removing litter from beaches ensures it doesn't get into the oceans and endanger the wildlife there.
- Ask your school to hold a fundraising event to raise money for an organization such as the WWF and help it protect whales.
- Start a blog about whales and the dangers they face. Educate as many people as you can.

GET EXPERIENCE

It is important to get some work experience if you want a career in conservation. Any form of work experience in wildlife care will help you decide the best way of using your talents in a future conservation career. Working for local zoos, charities, and conservation organizations as soon as you can will help give you the skills you need, too.

GET CONNECTED

Getting involved with a conservation group or charity can be really satisfying. You'll find some of the organizations you can join on page 47. Getting to know other people who are concerned about wildlife is a great way to find out what you can do to help endangered animals. Being involved with conservation organizations and charities now will also help you when you apply for jobs in the future. It will show that you have been interested in conservation from an early age.

CAREERS IN CONSERVATION

Conservation is a huge growth area today, as more and more people turn their focus to concerns about the environment. There are a huge number of conservation jobs available. Here is information about just some of them. You can find out about other conservation jobs on page 47 of this book.

▲ If you're someone who likes being outdoors, a wildlife manager could be the job for you.

WILDLIFE ECONOMIST

If you're good at math, perhaps you could become a wildlife economist. In this job, you would figure out the economic benefits of wildlife to individuals, as well as local and national businesses and governments. You could study the facts and figures related to tourist visits to marine reserves and find out what the economic benefits to whales' habitats are. This important job can make a huge difference to conservation decisions.

WILDLIFE MANAGER

Wildlife managers look after the animals in a natural area. In this role, you would monitor illegal hunting in a habitat. You would also keep track of the animal populations in the area and ensure that the habitat is suitable for the wildlife. You might also collect data and prepare research to help conservationists make decisions about how to help wildlife. A degree in environmental studies is usually needed.

WILDLIFE CONSULTANT

A wildlife consultant is a scientist who conducts research and surveys to provide advice on environmental issues. In this role, you might look at how plans for human activities in an area of ocean may affect the whales that live nearby or migrate through that area, for example. You could also create habitat restoration plans and check how successful they are when in place. Most wildlife consultants are wildlife biologists, so you would need a degree in biology.

PUBLIC RELATIONS OFFICER

If you like raising awareness about important issues, this could be the role for you. Public relations officers manage communications between organizations and the public. In this job, you could work for charities, wildlife organizations, and governments. You would raise awareness of wildlife issues. A degree in marketing is useful.

ENVIRONMENTAL SCIENTIST

If you become an environmental scientist, you will often gather vital information in the field. You may also conduct lab tests. For example, you might analyze water to check for pollution. You might test water to find the type, amount, and source of the pollution. An environmental science degree is usually required.

ENVIRONMENTAL LAWYER

Some environmental lawyers work for companies. In this role, you would advise the companies about the possible environmental effects they are having. That might include pollution they are causing through their practices, for example. If you worked for the government, you would help write laws that protect the environment and take people to court for breaking those laws. If you want to become an environmental lawyer, you will need a law degree with a specialization in environmental law.

◀ If you're good at science and would like to do something to help the world's wildlife and habitats, then you could consider training to be an environmental scientist, like the scientist on this research vessel.

GLOSSARY

adapted changed to suit an environment
atmosphere the layer of gases that surrounds Earth
baleen plates flexible comblike structures in the mouths of certain whales that are used to filter food from water
carbon emissions gases like carbon dioxide that are released into the atmosphere, often from burning fossil fuels
conservation protection of the planet
conservationists people who try to protect the planet
critically endangered facing an extremely high risk of extinction in the wild
echolocation a way some animals use sound to locate objects underwater
endangered facing a high risk of extinction
environment a natural place where plants and animals live
equator an imaginary line around the middle of Earth
extinction when a species dies out completely and no longer exists
feces solid waste passed from the body
fins flat body parts used by fish and whales to steer and move in water
flexible able to bend or move easily without breaking
food chain a system that shows how energy and nutrients pass from one organism to another
fossil fuels fuels formed from the remains of plants and animals that lived long ago
generations all the people or animals born and living at about the same time
geological related to Earth's structure
glacier a large mass of ice that moves slowly over land
Global Positioning System (GPS) a system that uses satellites in space that circle Earth and send back information. GPS can help people find locations on Earth
habitats the places in which plants and animals live
longlines extremely long fishing lines with many hooks
mammals types of animals that breathe air, give birth to live young, and usually have hair or fur
marine related to the sea or ocean
marine biologists scientists who study biology
marine reserves protected areas of the ocean where fishing and other activities are limited or banned
migrate to move from one place to another, often in search of food or to reproduce
military fighting forces
navigate to find the way from one place to another
nutrients substances that living things need to grow and stay healthy
plankton tiny floating organisms that are the base of ocean food chains
pollution harmful substances that make something dirty or dangerous to touch, eat, or drink
populations all the members of species living in a certain area
porpoises small marine mammals similar to dolphins but with shorter snouts and smaller bodies
predators animals that hunt and eat other animals
prey animals that are hunted and eaten by predators
reproduce to create young
sonar a system that uses sound waves to detect underwater objects and measure distances
species a group of living things that are similar and can reproduce
stranded left behind or stuck, often referring to whales on shore
sustainable can be relied upon for the foreseeable future

FIND OUT MORE

BOOKS

Eason, Sarah. *Saving the Shark* (Mission Survival: Saving Earth's Endangered Animals). Cheriton Children's Books, 2026.

Oseid, Kelsey. *Whales: An Illustrated Celebration*. Ten Speed Press, 2018.

Skerry, Brian. *The Secrets of Whales*. National Geographic, 2021.

WEBSITES

Discover more about careers that help fight climate change at:
www.bestcolleges.com/blog/climate-change-jobs

Hear directly from people working in conservation! Find out what they have to say about working in a career in conservation at:
www.conservation-careers.com/conservation-jobs-careers-advice/how-to-get-a-job-in-conservation

Discover the ultimate guide to careers in conservation at:
www.conservation-careers.com/15-key-conservation-jobs-ultimate-guide-for-conservation-job-seekers

Discover careers in environmental science at:
https://jobs.environmentalscience.org

Find out more about whales at:
www.fisheries.noaa.gov/whales

Learn more about whales at:
https://us.whales.org/kids-zone

INDEX

ABOUT THE AUTHOR

Katherine Eason has written many books about the natural world. She is passionate about conservation, and hopes this book inspires readers to make it their mission to help save the whale.